Lynn Chadwick

Universe Sculpture Series

Dr. J. P. Hodin **Chadwick**

Universe Books, Inc., New York

The Universe Sculpture Series is edited by Prof. Dr. A. M. Hammacher

Copyright 1961 in the Netherlands by Allert de Lange, Amsterdam
Library of Congress Catalog Card Number 60-14501
Typography and cover Otto Treumann, Gkf, AGI
Printed in the Netherlands by H. Veenman & Zonen N.V., Wageningen

Prelude

What is clearly evident from a study of modern art is the emergence of a new consciousness in which a genuine primitivism, i.e. mental states which in prehistoric and archaic art led to concrete mythical notions still active in the mentality of contemporary primitives, and a modern awareness derived from living in a world shaped by science and technology, are welded together to a unitary imagery. This new consciousness found its first realization in Cubism in which primitive elements of vision were blended with scientific geometric concepts and a new formative will took shape which aimed at the destruction of the post-Renaissance tradition and the creation of a style that corresponded to our own age. It follows logically that both the rational and the irrational have a part in this development; the machine-age civilization and the animistic-magic-vitalistic relationship to life. And the whole not as a result of pure speculation or mathematical calculation but expressive of a fight between the elementary forces in man and a one-sided abstract scientific way of thinking. A valid iconography is already crystallizing out of this fight, and its shapes which because of their strangeness could not be detected as such for decades are emerging like the skyline of an unknown townscape or a mountain chain in the early mist of a new morning. One can no longer speak of experimental art. This would mean to view the present through the spectacles of the past. The novel imagery is manifest as content in the work of many a leading artist of the mid-century. One of these is Lynn Chadwick.

Lynn Chadwick and his Generation

Without the mistakes
which lie in the assumption of morality
man would have remained an animal.
Friedrich Nietzsche

Man is descended
from some less highly organised form.
Charles Darwin

Each individual is born into a given phase of the evolution of human society. The world will present itself to him in its then specific historical aspect, economically, politically, and spiritually seen, and his existence will consist in grasping and solving the problems which it imposes upon him. This is his fate and these are his potentialities. Beyond the historical moment, however, there is what is eternal in Being, the ever-lasting flux in life and living. It is mirrored in man's reflections, in his myths and his imagery, in the way in which he gives shape to his surroundings, his hopes, his sorrows and his joys. The artist, the form-creating, image-making man, in expressing himself will give expression also to his generation and his own time. He will transcend both – given he is great enough – but even in this fruit of his genius the mark of the historic moment in which he lived will always be recognizable. Wilhelm Pinder said: "The artist cannot be transferred from his time. This means: the time into which he is born conditions the unfolding of his Being, indeed, his very Being itself. Thus the artist's Being depends on the time into which he is born. The artist's problems are born with him; they determine his destiny. This fact does not isolate the artist. On the contrary; it makes him belong to a group." (Das Problem der Generation in der Kunstgeschichte Europas, Berlin, 1926). Pinder attributes a style creating significance to this context of the generation.

"Generation is a stylistic value." The generation which was distinguished by the triumph of Lynn Chadwick at the Venice Biennale of 1956 had its definite characteristics. Born on the 24th November 1914 in Barnes, London, the year which swept away the old complacent world of the aristocratic-bourgeois alliance with its new powers and riches derived from the machine, Lynn Chadwick and his generation experienced nothing but wars, revolutions and the unsettled state of mind which was the result of the destruction of established cultural values, both religious and humanistic. The process of which these events represent only one phase began when science disrupted the foundations of the ancient Greco-Christian view of the world. With science triumphant, the European spirit had to enter the struggle for a new meaning of its cultural heritage, it had to grow new roots and find its soul in defying the rational. The age was not only agnostic, it was anti-religious. The sense of the miraculous quality of life, without which no work of art can be conceived, had to be recaptured. And it was recaptured by means which may have seemed to the representatives of previous generations unsuitable for such a conquest. They argued: "If there were such a thing as a fixed scientific scale of hardness by which the equation: ratio $\times$ emotion $=$ artistic expression could be determined in respect of each generation in the same way as minerals are determined according to their hardness, we should be able to attribute a co-efficient of hardness of each generation of artists which would define it with great accuracy. Yet, the secret of the creative quality would not thereby be revealed which expresses itself above all through the creator's detachment from the object of his production, particularly if it is an emotionally accentuated object. For "creating" is a spiritual and formative process, not the identification on the part of the artist with his emotions or with the emotions he desires to express. This was where in our century the Expressionists erred. That is why their own agitation and disappointments were more important to them than the life of the form which is the real subject of the history of art. This detachment, however, is something quite different from the "cold processes" of rationalist quality as we so frequently encounter them in contemporary art. It is also something entirely different from the conscious exclusion of all feeling, all intimacy and warmth, all emotionalism, with the exception of nega-tive emotions. In other words: Pessimism, nihilist Existentialism, dread, delirium of the ab-normal and the accidental – all this appeals to our time. Not so harmony, the unity embracing the opposing forces in the universe, humility, serenity and faith in the higher powers (not in the anthropomorphical sense), rejoicing in and devotion to life. All this would call for purity of heart and meditation; but our time lives on sensations and feverish activity which do not admit of contemplation. However, to quote Heinrich Wölfflin, "not all is possible at all times." And time determines the generation and its degree of hardness.

The generation which took part or grew up in the shadow of the second world war and matured during the disillusionment of the post-war period, the generation which substituted sex for love and deliberation for feeling; the generation of the age of psychoanalysis, political and social unrest, of materialistic massman, of cynicism and obscenity, with its scientific and techno-logical problems of outer space, who discuss the threat of atom bombs every day in the columns of their newspapers, preferred to shift the degree of hardness, i.e. the ratio of rationalism and feeling, so far in the direction of the ratio that they are in no danger of inflicting wounds on their soul because of inner "softness" (this has been the privilege of the generation of the first world war). The result was an impoverishment of the soul. If the generations of Shaftesbury and Rousseau had been imbued with landscape worship, ecstacy and sentimentality and that of the Romantics was one-sidedly emotional and melancholy, the generation of the Impressionists showed a marked change to the positive by their emphasis of light and sun, and the Fauvists by stressing la joie de vivre. With the Cubists, the geometric abstractionists, the Purists and the Constructivists, a progressively increasing congelation set in, so that there is hardly a greater contrast imaginable than that between the artist romanticizing nature and the geometric ab-stractionist. The Tachists and the Action painters again lapse from a need of opposition into the same error as did the Expressionists before, but with the difference that their goal is not the end product of the artistic intention but deliberately and exclusively the act of making as such, the nervous agitation during the working process. The result of this is the disastrous confusion which exists between creative activity and emotionalism, between art and nature, which we are witnessing today. We have seen that in the development of the last hundred years the degree of hardness in respect of the emotional element in art and in the artist has increased and no one can predict where this trend will meet its counter-thrust. Lynn Chadwick appears to us, in this context, a representative of a group of artists who, often precocious, always anti-hierarchic, unconcerned with morals, was raised to a dominant position under the modern motto that youth is a value *per se*. Autarchic youth, the erotic relationship between the sexes, the concept of the aggressive world of animal and man where toughness is a virtue, the rejection of idealism, biology in place of humanism. Never has a tree borne more rich fruit than that planted by Darwin and Nietzsche.

To judge this generation only from the ideological notions introduced by Darwinism into the philosophy of Nietzsche and adding the Kierkegaardian *Angst* arising from the nauseating feeling of insecurity, from man's loneliness without God, i.e. to judge this generation only as adherents to Existentialism whose pacemakers were Nietzsche and Kierkegaard, would be insufficient. Chadwick's generation has not only moved the accent from *Angst* to aggressiveness and defence – it is a self-conscious, proud, strong generation – it has also accepted an anti-historic attitude to life basing its artistic sensations exclusively on the directness of personal experience. Nothing is allowed to stand between them and life: neither convention nor prejudice, neither beauty nor a teaching code. They are rebels because they have an undiluted zest for life. They are explorers in the jungle of un-knowing. They are primitives in that they search for the primary sources of knowledge. This is primitive gesture which first entered modern art in the strivings of Gauguin and the Symbolists and, later, in a second wave, in that of Expressionism and Cubism – here significantly combined, as already mentioned, with a rational urge for construction and organization in complementing the philosophical tenets of Existentialism –, gives this generation its specific importance. It was Barbara Hepworth who said: "The work of the young artist today springs from innate impulses toward life, toward growth – impulses whose rhythms and structures have to do with the power and insistance of life. I see the present development in art as something opposed to any materialistic, anti-human or mechanistic direction of mind." Vitality is its sustaining concept.

Lynn Chadwick was an architectural draughtsman from 1933 to 1939. During the second world war he served as a pilot in the Fleet Air Arm. After being demobilized he continued at first his former work. But the urge for a more independent and creative activity, to which he had always inclined, became so strong that he decided to leave his profession and take a chance as a freelance designer. The evolution of his work in this stage was from architectural design to graphic design and, finally, to furniture designs. At the same time he was making mobiles which themselves had an evolution from wood to iron. He learned the technique of welding which enabled him to make the connecting links for his larger mobiles. This technique gave possibilities for producing the elements of the mobiles themselves and eventually for constructing the "stands" of mobiles such as we find in The Fisheater, which must be regarded as the forerunner of Chadwick's stabiles. The change from designer to sculptor was a gradual one, by way of mobiles, and unpremeditated.

After winning, in 1946, a competition for designs sponsored by the textile manufacturer Ascher, Chadwick came to an agreement with him to produce ten designs per year for the price of fifteen pounds each. With this "economic security" he entered his artistic career.

What did the sculptural scene look like at this moment? The material whose possibilities could be further explored was above all iron, the method that of direct welding or forging. In 1914 Marcel Duchamp exhibited a Bottle Rack in iron which he called "Ready Made." The Russians Vladimir Tatlin (Construction 1917), Kasimir Meduniezky (Construction 1919), and Alexander Rodschenko (Construction 1921), initiated a constructivist way. In 1928 Picasso produced an iron rod sculpture (Construction in Iron) and in 1930/31 a Construction in Wrought Iron; in 1932/33 Alberto Giacometti produced The Palace at 4 A.M., a construction with iron rods, wood, glass and string, with the help of which he conveyed not only a new space concept for sculpture but also a mythical implication. Julio Gonzales, Picasso's teacher in the technique of working in iron and reviver of the old Catalonian tradition of wrought iron work, combined with it a primitivist trend derived from Cubism (Angel, 1933, Head, Woman Combing Her Hair, 1936, Reclining Figure, 1936). Max Bill built in 1938/39 his Geometric Construction of 30 Identical Elements (iron rods).

The combination of a new material, a new technique and a primitivist content in form and message were important for the further development of modern sculpture. Alexander Calder, who was originally an engineer, explored the free play of natural movement for which he used wire, plain sheet iron, sheet aluminium, iron rods. He constructed mobiles (Steel Fish, 1934; Lobster Trap and Fish Tail, 1939; Thirteen Spines, 1940), stabiles (Black Beast, 1940; Morning Star, 1943) and, combined stabiles-mobiles (Le Plumeau Bleu, Bifurcated Tower, both 1950). All these instances introduced into the history of modern sculpture the notion of "a new iron age."

Another important element is the way in which the figure (human or animal) is rendered obliquely so that the appearances which are familiar regain their power of surprise as if seen for the first time. De Chirico introduced it in his metaphysical painting. Max Ernst made use of it (Anthropomorphic Figure, 1928; Loplop introduces a Young Girl, 1930), and so did Picasso (Figure Throwing a Stone, 1931; An Anatomy, 1933). This art of transformation with its impact on the subconscious layers of our mind, was further explored by Graham Sutherland (Standing Form against a Hedge, 1950; Three Standing Forms in a Garden, 1952) and to some extent also by Henry Moore (Reclining Figure, 1939, Standing Figure, 1950). In England it was above all Henry Moore who produced this spiritual climate which made sculpture a great adventure and enabled the young English generation, who had impressed themselves on international opinion at the Venice Biennale of 1952, to continue this remarkable revival of an art which had not had a local tradition in England for centuries. Reg Butler combined in his work both the idea of metamorphosis (Boy and Girl, 1950) and the use of welded and flattened iron, the manipulation of which he learned when he worked as a blacksmith during the war. Like Chadwick he started with architectural work. Already in 1953 Chadwick developed quite a personal style (Idiomorphic Beast) and, working parallel with the artists who represent this generation in this medium and in different countries (Robert Jacobsen, Berto Landera, David Smith, Theodore Roszak, Luciano Minguzzi, César and others), has become one of the most remarkable profiles among them.

The Unfolding of Lynn Chadwick's Work

*My purpose is
to tell of bodies which have been transformed
into shapes of a different kind.*
Ovid, The Metamorphoses

Chadwick produced altogether some sixty mobiles of different sizes during the years 1947–1952. The finest achievement in this group of work is the Fisheater (1951; ill. 1). The kinetic energy is provided by the wind. Mastery of the material combined with a fine sensibility for balance, movement and the harmony of large and small forms are its outstanding features. The chief structure is the elegant shape of a pair of pincers typical of crustaceans upheld by an elongated form in which the motif of teeth or hooks is repeating a similar motif inside the pincers which may also be seen as an open jaw. A group of small fish forms on the one end of the main structure is balanced by larger forms at the other end with two ball-shaped weights on long rods ensuring smooth movement. A third ball is added for the sake of the rhythm at the bottom of the elongated form between the supporting tripod. Other mobiles bear the titles The Dragon Fly (1951, The Tate Gallery), Endymion (1952), etc.
A combined mobile and stabile, or semi-mobile, which is called by Chadwick balanced sculpture, is to be found in Barley Fork (1952; ill. 2). (Only certain parts of the construction are movable and this only when pushed. In fact, every mobile consists of a fixed bearing part and one or several movable parts). Suggesting the character of an agricultural instrument it reveals a dynamic conception emphasizing the aggressive quality. This aggressiveness is already present in the Fisheater but in a more poetical way. Later on this element expressive of attack and

defense is intensified in various compositions of animals (Snapping Turtle, 1953/54, ill. 3; Beast I, 1955; The Seasons, 1956). It is this, together with the accent on sex, which makes one think of Chadwick's sculptures in Darwinian terms such as the struggle for existence, sexual selection, the survival of the fittest. The most outstanding of the balanced forms is The Inner Eye (1952; ill. 4) which is a structure consisting of a cell-shaped front plane with a round hole combined with a cage and four supporting legs. Through the hole a piece of glass fixed into a movable mounting is visible. The composition evokes a biomorphic connotation, ribs sheltering a soft inner organ, a shield-like exterior. The Inner Eye, however, could suggest also something more than a biological organ, and looking at The Stranger (ill. 5; 32), we may recognize therein a spiritual implication. The animal form suggests the human, a metamorphosis which by way of a shock gives the beholder a sensation of the unprecedented. The transitoriness of all living substance, be it man, animal or plant, is suggested as well. Although the titles are invented afterwards and the artist stresses that this method is not to give shape to a theme but to let a theme evolve by itself during the working, there is nevertheless an obvious link between titles and work, which may be indicative of inner motives driving the artist to express them in his sculptures. Quite naturally these seem to form themselves into series. Again, although there is no primary intention to produce series, a formal problem can show itself so interesting that it demands further investigation or formal exploitation until the fascination ebbs away. Thus we have after the series of mobiles, stabiles and balance sculptures the series of Beasts and other animals (Birds, Fishes, Dancing Figures, Encounters, Conjunctions, Winged Figures, the Moon of Alabama series (Sputnik-like objects), the series of Teddy Boy and Girl, Man and Woman (or boy and girl), a new variation of it, The Strangers, The Watchers. A definite trend from the purely biological towards a mythical and mystical conception of life is detectable in the works, the latest of which (some of the Teddy Boy and Girl compositions) show ritual, even magic or exorcizing gestures. In animal shapes this tendency was already evident in a composition such as Encounter (1955; ill. 6). If we take the sequence: Encounter, then (ritual) Dance, then Conjunction and, finally, those sculptures which seem to represent the carnal union of two (Two Dancing Figures II, 1955/56 (ill. 7), or Two Winged Figures, 1955), we may trace Darwinism in them but we may also find the evolution of a life concept which has deeper roots than that. And here the method of working and the inner driving force, the unconscious motivation meet. The experiencing with a sense which is not conceptual, the working without a preconceived scheme which would in fact destroy intuition and empathy, the use of pieces of material lying about in the studio whereby the accidental is involved but later controlled by the imagination (the first winged figure, for instance, Dance, 1955, ill. 8, came about in this way, the artist using a piece of material as a "wing," leading further to other winged figures that are not birds but something going beyond the notion of man or bird) – they all speak of what Lévy-Brühl called "*participation mystique*" in the experience of the primitives, the mystical participation in the phenomenon of life in us and around us. Of the art of the primitives he said that they are "the plastic expression of the most sacred collective imagery, like certain myths whose poetic, and certain institutions, whose social outflow they are. If often art attempts to render creatures which are half animal, half man, it wants thereby to express the mysterious union of human and animal form in these creatures which are the object – treated with shy reverence – of that imagery." (L'Âme primitive).

To a certain extent this is applicable to Chadwick's work and experiencing too. We say to a certain extent for our world of the second industrial revolution (Cybernatics) and of hyper-trophic cerebralism makes the struggle understandable between the Darwinian scientific notions and those of the mysticism and symbolism of primitive man (which are still present in the deepest layers of our consciousness), the struggle or, rather, the process of reconciliation which takes place in the mind of this artist as a representative of our time and his generation.

The Darwinian notion is indeed present in Chadwick's work: the evolution of life from lower to higher animal forms and the metamorphical use made of them in the work of the artist. The insectomania of our time, for instance, as manifested by Massin, was introduced in England by Graham Sutherland and Reg Butler. James Ensor had already expressed similar ideas and Franz Kafka's short story "The Transformation" – the transformation of man into a lower living or-ganism – is the literary embodiment of this nightmarish thought. The Industrial Age has of course shown special interest in the life of the termites, wasps, bees and ants, i.e. in the forms of state organizations in the animal world. The enlarged biting apparatus, the prickly limbs and armor of the insects and crustacea, the jaws, teeth, claws, fangs and horns of the larger animals, the spikes and thorns of the plants, the knife-like, nail-like and dagger-like forms oc-curring in modern art, are symbols of aggressiveness. Here the Darwinian notion is brought into relation with the condition of our age, here the desperate generation comes into its own. (John W. Aldrige, After the Lost Generation, London, 1959). The aggressive element is apparent also in the Teddy Boy and Girl compositions, this time aggressive in the ideological sense – for designated as Teddies is a social "group" which, however, will have nothing to do with any class distinctions and which, while recruiting its adherents from working-class adolescents, finds sympathizers among the intelligentsia, and the Sartre-accentuated Existentialist Nihilist of the Boulevard St. Germain quarter of Paris is the prototype especially among the young artists who also cannot easily be categorized (John Osborne, Look Back in Anger). The "Teddy Boy" is a rebellious, dandy-minded person living mentally at the periphery of society, who often makes money easily. He underlines his individuality by the emphasis on the "archaic" elements in his dress (the style of the Edwardian era), is anarchistic-provocative, an a-social element in the great social revolution, who cannot assume responsibility, who is marked by an exaggerated egocentric drive for freedom, who, though dependent on society, dissociates himself from it and exploits it, a "libertine" without education who finds his ideal in sexual promiscuity, film, jazz and jitterbug.

But just as present in Chadwick's work as the Darwinian notion is that of the *participation mystique*. If a figure such as Stranger II, 1956 (ill. 9), suggests the Egyptian God Set with the Head of the Typonian Animal or if the two figures of Encounter VI (1956/57; ill. 10) meet like monumental towers reminiscent of Gothic architecture in its rising upward, these are not stylistic derivations but the expression of a mentality tending toward the primary and the mythical in the same way as Constantin Brancusi tried to express the quality of the fabulous in his bird composition Maiastra or Giacometti when producing analogies to Etruscan emaciated miniature figures gave form to the idea of soul-less mass-man. Encounter VIII (1957; ill. 11) is the strange evocation of a first meeting between two people in animal shape, Conjunction (1953; ill. 12) is the union of two beings, reminding us not only of the ritual performed by birds and animals when courting, movements which were reproduced by the primitives in their dances, but of the uniqueness of the situation when two strange personages meet and involve each other. It touches upon the mystery of life. And life is what Chadwick is concerned with, the life-force itself. And not alone the fact of its existence but its meaning, the strangeness of its dynamics. That is what gripped Chadwick and that is what he expressed in his personal work. Personal it is both in its idea and in its form language, and it became so immediately after the initial period of mobiles and stabiles. As this lasted only five years, and Chadwick had worked with solid forms only two years before he received the great international sculpture prize in Venice, we have to see in his art — which since then has become a source of influence itself — a development of extraordinary rapidity and maturity. One reason for this is that he belongs to a generation which, not having been burdened down by any considerations of tradition in style and technique, achieves a novel vision without having to struggle against the conventional. Of the series the largest hitherto is that of the Beast, (Beast XVIII, 1959, ill. 13). There are so far thirty (1946–60). In them Chadwick found a medium by which to express some basic attitudes to life characteristic of the second generation of "hollow men." In them he represented also the unity of all living creatures in their determinism as well as their acceptance or defiance of fate. In them (and this is true also of the other series) he found a way of evolving his extraordinary gift of variation of a given form. In them he found a means of expressing in his style the elementary positions of standing, sitting, moving or lying. His metamorphosed human figures (the Encounters, of which there are now twenty-two, the Conjunctions, of which there are twelve, the Dancing Figures, of which there are twenty four, the Winged Figures, of which there are twelve, the Teddy Boy and Girl (Man and Woman, Boy and Girl) of which there are sixteen, and the group of Strangers (sixteen) and Watchers (eight), again express primary moods and attitudes of life. Their formal development is closely tied up with the technique involved. This technique imposes the structure and the tectonic quality of his sculptures and defines also its own limitations. The artist once said: "I emphasize the character which the technique gives. There are limitations – I stress the character imposed by the limitations." And again: "I believe that it is necessary for the artist to have a feeling for the method in which he works, whatever his medium. I am pleased if the iron forms I make have a sort of organic reality, as if they were the logical expression of the materials which I use. I do not expect much vitality in my work unless this is so." (The New Decade. Edited by Andrew Carnduff Ritchie). Chadwick prefers the straight to the curved lines. Hence the angularity of the shapes, the often crystalline forms employed. They are a direct aspect of the linear rods welded together which constitute the armature of the figures. They are sometimes triangular in plan, tetrahedral in space or irregular according to the large planes they have to contain or the patterns they are designed to form on their surface. In Idiomorphic Beast (1953; ill. 14) the large forms are so densely filled in with decorative linear elements (welded together) that a closed surface appears. This is the first example of Chadwick's work of a solid figure, crystalline in this case, after having produced exclusively linear, skeleton- and armature-like compositions. From 1954 onward, beginning with Two Dancing Figures (ill. 15) of that year, he employed for the first time a compound or gypsum and iron filing (used in the industry for the bases of heavy machinery) which he worked with a spatula and with which the whole figure was also filled inside. Later on, finding the figures too heavy, he left them hollow. He soon discovered that the iron bars had decorative and also expressive qualities like nerves on leaves or furrows on plaved fields and he left them as visible linear elements in the compound. Here they form various patterns which are rhythmic and dynamic in their effect. They are either parallel but standing at an angle to the lines limiting the large forms (Conjunction II, 1954), or they are parallel to the edges of the figure (Maquette for Teddy Boy and Girl II, 1957; ill. 16), or they form a multiple triangular ray-like pattern (Encounter 1955) a rhomboid pattern (Dance V, 1955), a diagonal pattern (Encounter VI, 1956/57), or they are arranged centrifugally (Rock, 1955); they suggest ribs (Beast IX, 1956; ill. 17), a mane (Beast I, 1955), or a wing (Stranger VII, 1959); they are shaped in low or high relief (Dance V, 1959).

The technical and the decorative devices would, however, be insufficient to constitute a work of art for Chadwick. Therefore, writing once that it is the feeling of works of art which inspires him rather than the technical execution, he said of his own sculpture: "I have not felt the need to follow a style or even for that matter to evolve a style of my own, other than what I hope is a continuity of feeling." (Letter to the author of February 6th, 1956). All Chadwick's figures of Beasts stand on four stilt-like legs (forged bars). When composing single metamorphosed human figures – i.e. all Watchers and Strangers – they either stand on three legs (Dance, 1955; Watchers, 1959; Stranger V, 1959; ill. 18) or on two legs cemented into a low base (Stranger VII, 1959; Watcher II, 1959; ill. 19). The Watchers and Strangers have square-shaped heads large in relation to the bodies (stylistically related to the conception of the Easter Island sculptures) and expressive of their peculiar function and psychological characteristics. They are solitary figures outside the social communication represented in the double figures (Strangers III, 1959, ill. 20; Strangers IV, 1959, ill. 21). The double figures created a problem in that they had to be connected on one point or plane so that they form one body and are carried by four legs like single animals. Some of these connecting bridges suggest the act of copulation (Encounter, 1955, or Dance, 1955; Maquette for Two Winged Figures, 1955; Two Dancing Figures II, 1955/56; Conjunction VII, 1959; ill. 22); some are joined at the hip (Two Dancing Figures VI, 1955), some in a diagonal way (Maquette for Teddy Boy and Girl III, 1957), some form one large but articulated shape, a collective body (Encounter X, 1959; ill. 23), reminding us of the sculptural solution which Armitage found for his representations of several figures – a group, the mass – in one many-headed form. The heads and also the hands of Chadwick's figures are small and abstracted. They have their ancestors (Picasso, Moore, Giacometti, archaic art); they are stylized in a geometric way without losing their organic quality. They even acquire a suggestive quality loaded with emotional power without attempting to be symbolic. They are, formally seen, a necessary consequence of the bodies being also abstracted and to a great extent geometrized. In his double figure Chadwick confronts either two triangular or rhomboid shapes (Encounter, 1955), or a triangular with a square shape (Teddy Boy and Girl, 1955 (ill. 24); Maquette for Teddy Boy and Girl II, 1957; Encounter VI, 1956/57).

In the Seasons (1955; ill. 25) a triangular shape is opposed to an antler- or bush-like feature, the lines of which leap out in all directions into the infinite. The title here is quite accidental and used only to comply with a theme suggested by the Contemporary Art Society for an exhibition called "The Seasons" (London, 1956). Some figures approximate the human form (the series of Two Dancing Figures, I/II, 1954–1956, or Maquette for Two Winged Figures, 1955; ill. 26), but realism is never aimed at. Realism is in fact the enemy of any spiritual concept. It excludes the human element which is the experiencing self of the artist in surrendering it to a fictitious objectivity. Sometimes an amorphous element enters in the handling of the solid compound (Dance, 1955; Watcher, 1959), but it is confined in the limits of a geometric shape. It is here that Chadwick comes nearest to modeling, a method which he in fact avoided as much as the direct carving in stone or wood. In this he and his generation were quite decidedly anti-tra-ditionalist. Having touched upon the problem of Realism, we can say of its extreme opposite, Abstraction, that Chadwick, although having produced abstract shapes, found them inadequate for the expression of his inner experiences.

The surfaces of his works – with the exception of the mobiles and constructions and the fol-lowing beaten shapes with limbs and connections – i.e. the surfaces of his solid forms are rough, displaying a patina derived from the same material of which the compound is made. Exposed to the wet, the fine gray or black changes to a rusty color caused by the iron filings, stressing the antagonism to any precious, polished or otherwise "beautiful" quality. They have however, an aesthetic character of their own. The surfaces may vary between a golden yellow, darkgray or black. On the whole they are treated so as to intensify the expressive qualities of the sculp-tures. Until recently, Chadwick's human figures had a "private" character; in spite of their monumental size they were not intended for the open space. Only recently (1958) were such compositions undertaken to be placed out of doors (The Watchers, 1960; ill. 27 en 28). In 1957 Chadwick started to produce works in bronze. Three or four casts are taken from an original which is not of plaster but the usual solid figure made of a welded iron frame and filled with compound. Chadwick rarely works from sketches but directly with the welding machine. An idea emerges, taken shape, changes, until it reaches a final stage. The drawings and washes (ill. 29, 30 and 31) which he produces are works in their own right, variations on the main themes of his sculptured opus.

Conclusion

"I do not analyze my work intellectually. Chadwick wrote. When I start to work I wait till I feel what I want to do; and I know how I am working by the presence or lack of a rhythmic impulse. I think that to attempt to analyze the ability to draw ideas from their subconscious sources would almost certainly interfere with that ability." (The New Decade).

Never before in the history of art has the artist stood so lonely amidst the bewildering wealth of life, amidst decaying spiritual concepts, with only a slow, very slow crystallization of new valid concepts. In the course of the disintegration of an age-old moral code, of religious beliefs and a sheltered poetry of Being, scientific notions and methods have destroyed the confidence in instinct, technology has taken the place of meditation. A hectic activity stigmatizes our age, technically, economically, politically. It is an age of breathtaking rhythm. Intellectually the national and continental segmentation of culture is breaking down, ceding place to a global consciousness. In time our knowledge reaches deep into the prehistoric geological sphere; in space man is on the verge of exploring empirically the universe. In art the form-consciousness of the whole of mankind throughout all the ages has become our heritage. But the modern artist is facing life empty-handed, without the compass of established creeds. Even the imagery of cave-man was expressive of a definite attitude to life in which it had its practical function. The sculptures of Autun are the visible presence of an accepted notion of Being. The carver who shaped the Cycladian amulets, the artist who filled the inner and outer spaces of the Borobudu with sacred figures, the master of the statuary of the lateral portals of Chartres, the painters of Zen – they all had the spiritual certainty which our age is still withholding from our feverishly restless consciousness. Only psychology is with us – no philosophy, no religious conviction. And the miracle of life. Never before in man's history has the artist stood so empty-handed and lonely before creation. That is why he has to turn his back on the life-force itsel- and strip himself of any consciousness to re-discover in the instinct the elemental syllables of a new language.

Bibliography

Herbert Read,	*Contemporary British Art*. Penguin Books, Harmondswirth 1951.
E. H. Ramsden,	*Sculpture: Theme and Variations*. Lund Humphries, London, 1953.
Andrew Carnduff Ritchie,	*The New Decade*. 22 European Painters and Sculptors. The Museum of Modern Art, New York, 1955.
Carola Giedion-Welcker,	*Contemporary Sculpture*. An Evolution in Volume and Space. Faber and Faber, London, 1956.
J. P. Hodin,	*Contemporary English Sculpture: Recent Trends and Their Origin*, In: *The Dilemma of Being Modern*. Routledge and Kegan Paul, London, 1956.
J. P. Hodin,	*La Sculpture Anglaise*, In: *Encyclopédie de l'Art International Contemporain*. Prisme des Arts, Edition d'Art et Industrie, Paris, 1958.
Herbert Read,	*Great Britain*, In: *Art Since 1945*. Thames and Hudson, London, 1958. (Original German Edition: Neue Kunst nach 1945, Edited by Will Grohmann. M. DuMont Schauberg, Cologne. American Edition, Harry N. Abrams, New York. Italian Edition: L'Arte Dopo Il 1945, Il Saggiatore, Milan.
Charles McCurdy (Editor),	*Modern Art*. A Pictorial Anthology. The Macmillan Company, New York, 1958. Chapter: Sculpture: An International Survey, 1852–1956, by A. L. Chanin.

| Michel Seuphor, | *The Sculpture of this Century*. Zwemmer, London, 1960. Present-Day Sculpture in Great Britain |

Catalogues

Herbert Read,	*Recent (British) Sculpture*. XXVIth Biennale, Venice. 1952.
Werner Schmalenbach,	*Lynn Chadwick*. Kenneth Armitage–Lynn Chadwick Exhibition, Kestner Gesellschaft, Hannover, April–May, 1960.
Robert Melville,	*Lynn Chadwick*, XXVIIIth Biennale, Venice, 1956. (Reprinted in the catalogues of the exhibitions listed under one-man shows, 1956/57).
Bernard Dorival,	*Preface*. Musée National d'Art Moderne, Paris, 1957.
Edouard Trier,	*Einführung*. 11. *Documenta '59*. Skulptur. Verlag M. DuMont Schauberg, Köln, 1959.

Monographs

| Herbert Read, | *Lynn Chadwick*. 23 pp. text. (English and German) and 24 plates. Bodensee-Verlag, Amriswil, Switzerland, 1958. |

Statements by the Artist

In: Andrew Carnduff Ritchie, *The New Decade*. 22 European Painters and Sculptors. The Museum of Modern Art, New York, 1955.

Articles

| J. P. Hodin | Testimonianza sulla scultura inglese attuale. Sele Arte, Florence, November–December, 1953. |

J. P. Hodin	The XXVIIIth Venice Biennale. The Norseman, Vol. XIV, No. 5, London, September–October, 1956.
J. P. Hodin	Den 28ie Biennale I Venedig. Konstperspektiv XII, No. 3, Göteborg, 1956.
J. P. Hodin	*The Venice Biennale*. Arts, New York, August 1956.
J. P. Hodin	*Lynn Chadwick*. Das Werk, No. 3, March, 1957.
J. P. Hodin	Twee Engelse Kunstenaars, Kroniek van Kunst en Kultuur, XVII, No. 3, Amsterdam, March 1957.
J. P. Hodin	*The Triumph of Lynn Chadwick*. Art News and Review, Vol. IX, No. 13, London, July, 1957.
Robert Melville	*Lynn Chadwick*. Quadrum II, Brussels, 1956.
Robert Melville	Visite à Lynn Chadwick. L'Oeil No. 26, Paris, 1957.
Aleksander Wojciechowski	Sztuka wielkiego niepokojn. Przeglad Artystyczny, No. 3, May-June 1957, Warsaw.
Theo Crosby	*Lynn Chadwick*. Architectural Design, London, April 1959.
Udo Kultermann	Englische Plastik der Gegenwart. Das Kunstwerk, Baden-Baden, 7/XII, January, 1959.
Suzanne Lombard	*Lynn Chadwick*. Les Beaux-Arts, Brussels, 1957.
Guy Playfair	*Lynn Chadwick, Sculptor in Metal*. Motif No. 4, London, March, 1960.

Works in public collections

The Tate Gallery, London
The British Council, London
The Arts Council of Great Britain
The Victoria and Albert Museum, London
Bristol Art Gallery
Brighton Art Gallery
Pembroke College, Oxford
National Gallery of Canada, Ottawa
National Gallery of South Australia, Adelaide
Museum of Modern Art, New York
Carnegie Institute, Pittsburgh
University of Michigan
Albright Art Gallery, Buffalo
Chicago Art Institute
Institute de Artes Contemporáneas, Lima
Sécrétariat d'Etat aux Arts et Lettres (Musée National d'Art Moderne, Paris)
Boymans Museum, Rotterdam
Municipality of Recklinghausen
The Art Gallery, Göteborg
Musées Royaux des Beaux-Arts de Belgique, Brussels
Ministero della Pubblica Instructione, Italy (Gallerie d'Arte Moderna, Roma)
Museo Civico di Torino
Staatliche Graphische Sammlung, Munich

Biography

1914	November 24. Born at Barnes, London.
	Studies at the Merchant Taylor School of Architecture.
1933–39	Works in various architectural firms in London.
1941	Visits New York and Detroit.
1941–44	Pilot in the Fleet Air Arm.
1944–46	Works with architects in London.
1946	Wins a competition for textile designs arranged by the firm of Ascher in London.
1947–52	Produces textile, furniture and architectural designs for exhibitions.
	Experiments with mobiles inspired by the architect Rodney Thomas.
1948–58	Lives in Upper Coberley, Gloucestershire.
1951	Visits to Toronto and New York.
1952	Visits Paris.
1953	Produces the first balanced sculptures.
	Honorable mention at the International Competition for the Monument of the Unknown Political Prisoner, London.
1955	Visits Athens.
1956	Wins the great international prize for sculpture at the XXVIIIth Biennale of Venice.
	Visits Venice, Amsterdam, Brussels.
1956–57–58	Visits Menerbes, Provence.
1957	Visits Zürich.
1958	(January) Visits Munich and Zürich.
1958	(September) Moves to Lypiatt Park near Stroud, Gloucestershire.
1959	Wins the first prize in the IIIrd International "Bronzetto" Competition (small bronzes) in Padua.
	Visits Zürich and Kassel.

Exhibitions

One-Man Shows

1950   Gimpel Fils Gallery, London
1952   Gimpel Fils Gallery, London
1956   XXVIIIth Biennale, Venice. In 1956/57 this exhibition was shown in the following Museums: Wiener Sezession, Vienna; Städtische Galerie (Lenbach-Galerie), Munich; Musée National d'Art Moderne, Paris; Stedelijk Museum, Amsterdam; Palais des Beaux-Arts, Brussels; Arts Council, London.
1957   Saidenberg Gallery, New York
1958   Galerie Daniel Cordier, Paris
1959   Galerie Charles Lienhard, Zürich
        Galerie Daniel Cordier, Frankfurt
1960   Kestner Gesellschaft, Hanover
        Museum, Ulm
        Städtisches Kunstmuseum, Duisburg
        Haus am Waldsee, Berlin
        Städtische Kunstsammlungen, Nuremberg
        Konsthallen, Gothenburg
        Galerie M. M. Knödler, Paris

Group Exhibitions

1947   The first mobile shown at the Building Trades Exhibition, London
1948   Commissioned to produce mobiles at a Trades exhibition, London
1949   Gimpel Fils Gallery, London
1951   2nd International Open-Air Exhibition of Sculpture, Battersea Park, London
        International Exhibition, Riverside Gallery, New York
        "South Bank" Exhibition, Festival of Britain, London
1952   "Recent Sculpture" Exhibition, XXVIth Biennale, Venice
        Galerie de France, Paris
1953   "The Unknown Political Prisoner" Exhibition, Tate Gallery, London
        9th Salon de Mai, Paris

	2nd International Open-Air Exhibition, Middleheim-Park, Antwerp
	"Sculpture in the Home" Exhibition in London and other towns in Great Britain
1954	"British Painting and Sculpture" Exhibition, Whitechapel Art Gallery, London
	3rd International Open-Air Exhibition, Holland-Park, London
1955	Documenta I, Exhibition, Kassel
	"Eisenplastik" Exhibition, Kunsthalle, Berne
	"The New Decade" Exhibition, Museum of Modern Art, New York; Minneapolis, Los Angeles; San Francisco
1955/56	"Young British Sculptors" Exhibition. In Germany: Munich, Stuttgart, Freiburg, Karlsruhe, Recklinghausen, Düsseldorf; In Holland: Rotterdam
1956	International Exhibition David Jones Gallery, Sidney
	"The Seasons" Exhibition, Tate Gallery, London
	International Open-Air Exhibition, Musée Rodin, Paris
	British Kunst 1900–1955, Exhibition, Kunstforeningen, Copenhagen
1956/57	"Young British Sculptors" Exhibition in Stockholm and other towns in Sweden
1957	4th International Open-Air Exhibition, Holland Park, London
	3rd International Open-Air Exhibition, Middleheim-Park, Antwerp
	"Ten Young British Sculptors" Exhibition, 4th Biennale, Sao Paulo
	International Exhibition of Drawings, Freunde junger Kunst, Düsseldorf
1958	"50 Ans d'Art Moderne", World Exhibition, Brussels
	"Contemporary British Painting and Sculpture" Exhibition, British Embassy, Brussels
	"Four British Artists" (Moore, Sutherland, Chadwick, Armitage), Galleria BLU, Milano
1958/59	"Ten Young British Sculptors" Exhibition, Museo de Arte Moderna, Rio de Janeiro; Museo Nacional de Bellas Artes, Buenos Aires, Museo de Arte Moderna, Montevideo; Instituto de Artes Plasticas, Santiago; Instituto de Artes Contemporaneas, Lima; Museo de Bellas Artes, Caracas
	International Exhibition of Sculptor's Drawings, Duisburg, Fübingen Saarbrücken.
1959	Documenta II, Kassel
	5th International Biennale of Sculpture, Middleheim-Park, Antwerp
1960	Sculpture in the Open Air, Battersea Park, London
	Contemporary British Sculpture Exhibition organized by the Arts Council in various towns in Great Britain.

2 **Fourche à orge** 1952   53 cm
  Barley Fork $10\frac{3}{4}''$
  Gerstengabel
  Gerstvork
  Rastrillo de cebada

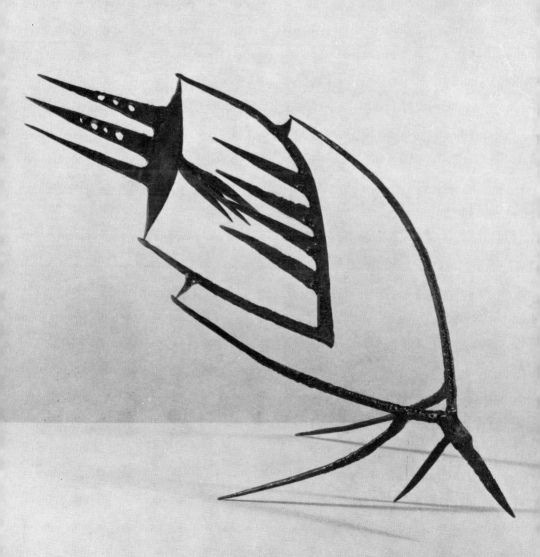

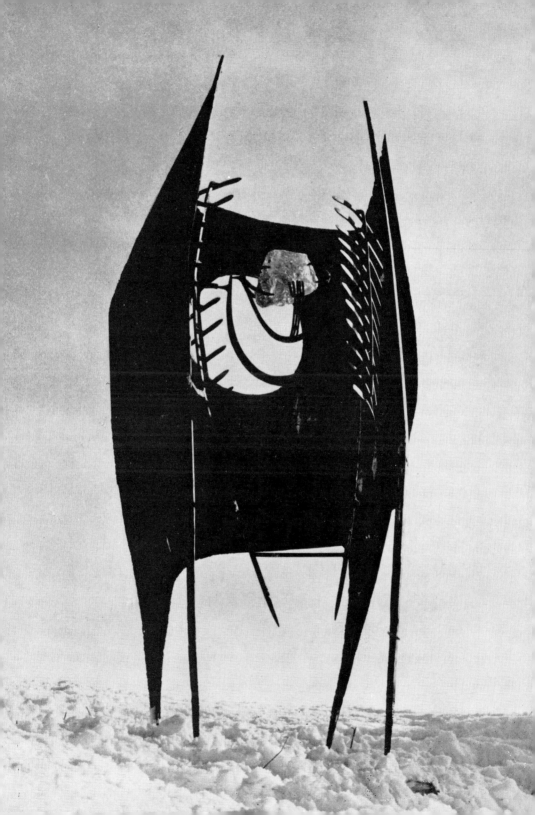

5 **L'Étranger**   1954   76 cm
  The Stranger   30″
  Fremder
  De vreemdeling
  El extranjero

43513

8 **Danse** 1955   57 cm
  Dance   22½″
  Tanz
  Dans
  Baile

9 **Étranger II** 1956 110,5 cm
   Stranger II 43½"
   Fremder II
   Vreemdeling II
   Extranjero

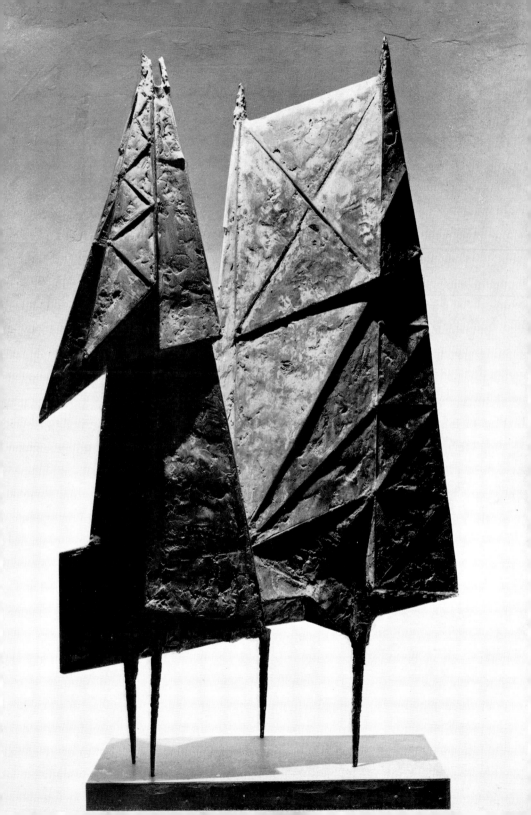

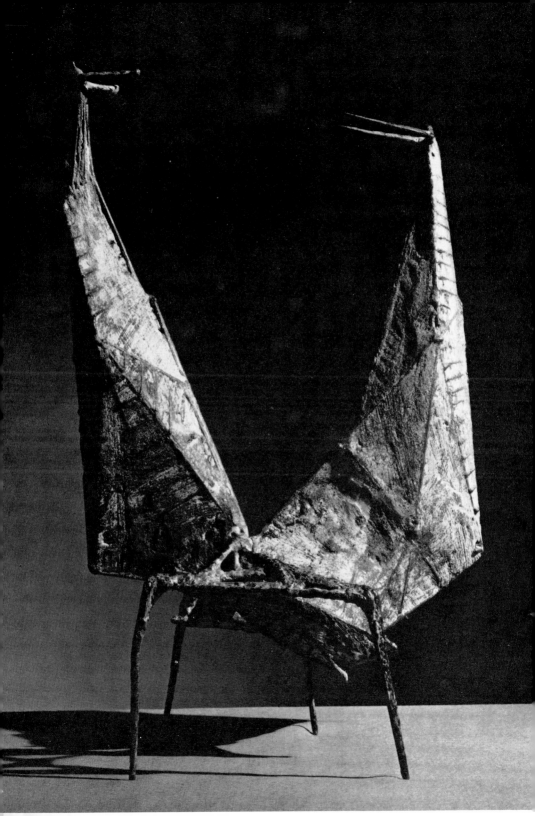

13 **Animaux sauvages XVIII**   1959   28,5 cm
   Beasts XVIII   11¼″
   Wilde Tiere XVIII
   Beesten XVIII
   Fieras

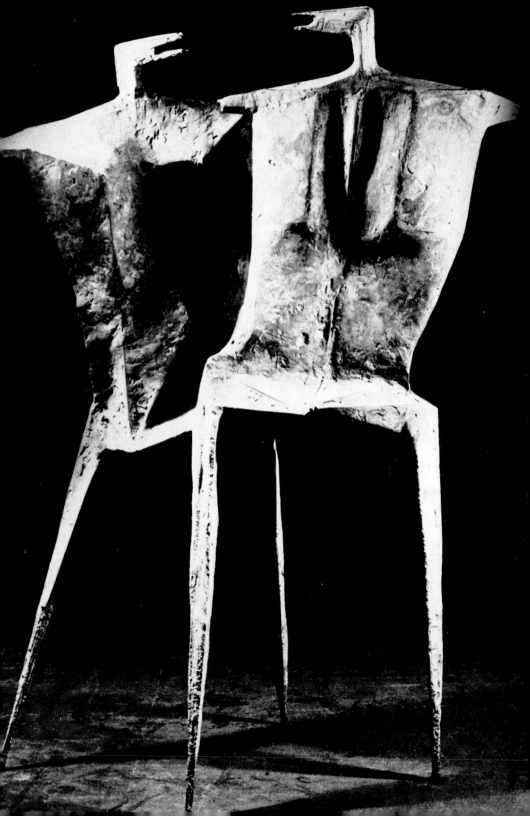

18 **Etranger V** 1959 48,5 cm
   Stranger V 19″
   Fremder V
   Vreemdeling V
   Extranjero

20 **Etrangers III**   1959   230 cm
   Strangers III   90″
   Fremder III
   Vreemdelingen III
   Extranjeros

21 **Etrangers IV** 1959 61,5 cm
 Strangers IV 24¼″
 Fremder IV
 Vreemdelingen IV
 Extranjeros

24 **Teddy Boy et jeune fille** 1955 190,5 cm
   Teddy Boy and Girl 75″
   Teddy Boy und Mädchen
   Teddy Boy met meisje
   Teddy Boy y una muchacha

26 **Maquette pour deux figures ailées**   1955   57 cm
   Maquette for Two Winged Figures   22½"
   Maquette für Zwei geflügelte Figuren
   Ontwerp voor twee gevleugelde figuren
   Esbozo para dos figuras aladas

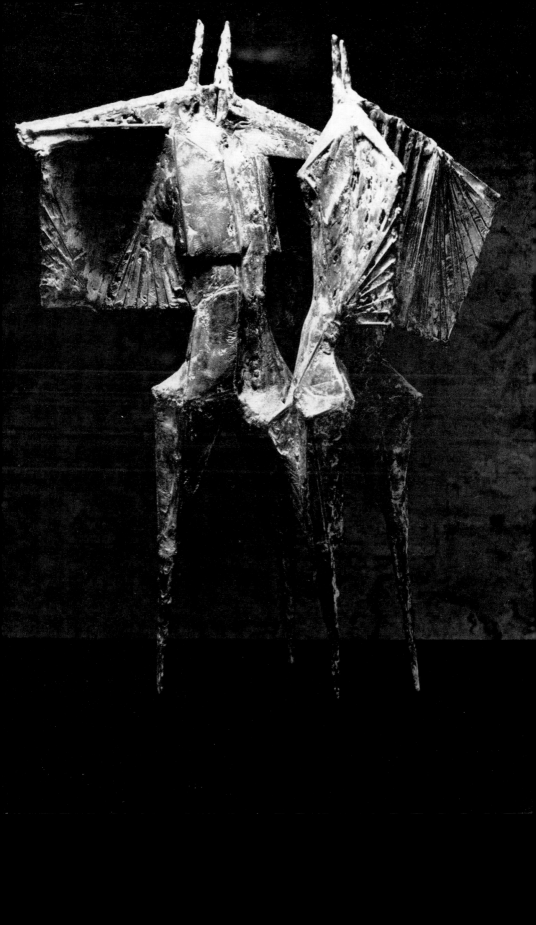

27 **Gardien** 1959 85 cm
   Watcher 32½″
   Wächter
   Wachter
   Vigilante

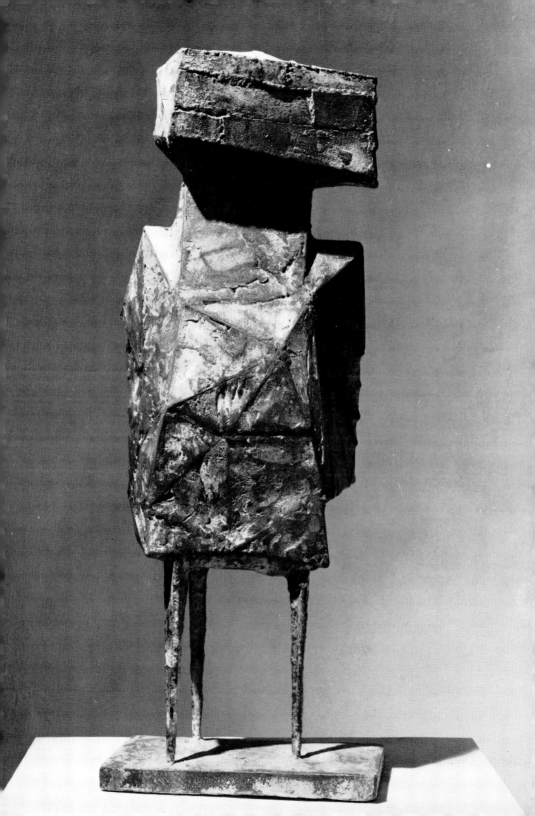

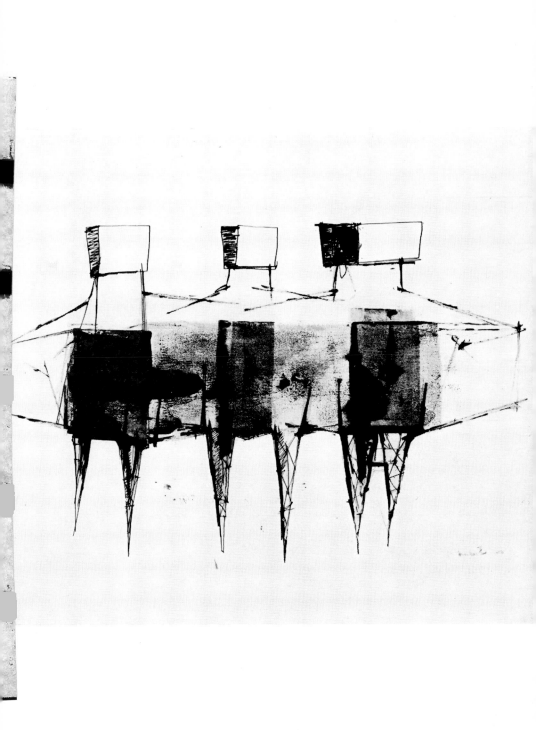

30 **Animal**   dessin   plume et gouache   1956 collection Dr. J. P. Hodin, London
   Beast   drawing   pen and wash
   Tier   Zeichnung Feder und Wasserfarbe
   Beest   tekening   pen en waterverf
  Animal   dibujo   pluma y aguada   Colección Dr. J. P. Hodin, Londres

chadwick 56.

Chadwick 57.

32 **Etranger VII**   1959   78 cm
   Stranger VII $32\frac{3}{4}''$
   Fremder VII
   Vreemdeling VII
   Extranjero